# PACHYCEPHALOSAURUS

## AND OTHER BONE-HEADED PLANT-EATERS

**Prehistoric World**

# PACHYCEPHALOSAURUS
## AND OTHER BONE-HEADED PLANT-EATERS

VIRGINIA
SCHOMP

*BENCHMARK BOOKS*

MARSHALL CAVENDISH
NEW YORK

DINOSAURS LIVED MILLIONS OF YEARS AGO. EVERYTHING WE KNOW ABOUT THEM—HOW THEY LOOKED, WALKED, ATE, FOUGHT, MATED, AND RAISED THEIR YOUNG—COMES FROM EDUCATED GUESSES BY THE SCIENTISTS WHO DISCOVER AND STUDY FOSSILS. THE INFORMATION IN THIS BOOK IS BASED ON WHAT MOST SCIENTISTS BELIEVE RIGHT NOW. TOMORROW OR NEXT WEEK OR NEXT YEAR, NEW DISCOVERIES COULD LEAD TO NEW IDEAS. SO KEEP YOUR EYES AND EARS OPEN FOR NEWS FLASHES FROM THE PREHISTORIC WORLD!

Benchmark Books
Marshall Cavendish
99 White Plains Road
Tarrytown, New York 10591-9001
www.marshallcavendish.com

© Marshall Cavendish Corporation 2004

Library of Congress Cataloging-in-Publication Data

Schomp, Virginia.
  Pachycephalosaurus and other bone-headed plant-eaters / by Virginia Schomp.
     p. cm. — (Prehistoric world)
Summary: Describes the physical characteristics and behavior of Pachycephalosaurus
and other bone-headed plant-eating dinosaurs.
Includes bibliographical references and index.
  ISBN 0-7614-1542-4
  1. Pachycephalosaurus—Juvenile literature. [1. Pachycephalosaurus. 2.Dinosaurs.]  I. Title.
  QE862.O65P33 2004
  567.914—dc21
                        2003000744

Front cover: Two *Pachycephalosaurus*          Back cover: *Goyocephale*          Pages 2–3: *Prenocephale*

Cover illustration: The Natural History Museum, London / Orbis

The illustrations and photographs in this book are used by permission and through the courtesy of:
*Marshall Cavendish Corporation:* 2-3, 8-9, 10, 17, 18, 19, 20-21, 24, back cover. *The Natural History Museum, London:* 13, 23; John Sibbick, 15; Orbis, 16, 22.

Map and Dinosaur Family Tree by Robert Romagnoli

Printed in China
1 3 5 6 4 2

For Darius and Brendan Dromazos

# Contents

# THE BATTLING BONE-HEADS

An odd-looking dinosaur gobbles up greens on a North American mountain slope. It is a *Pachycephalosaurus*—the biggest of the bone-heads. And it is about to demonstrate how it got its name.

A young *Albertosaurus* creeps near. The hungry meat-eater would enjoy a meal of fresh *Pachycephalosaurus*. But as the predator attacks, the bone-headed dinosaur lowers its head and charges. Its thick skull slams the meat-eater's side like a battering ram. The *Albertosaurus* topples, and the scared but safe bone-head keeps on running.

A Pachycephalosaurus *uses its thick skull to knock over a dangerous young meat-eating dinosaur.*

Bone-heads. Thick-heads. Helmet-heads. These are a few of the names used for the group of dinosaurs called pachycephalosaurs. The bone-heads were small to medium-sized plant-eaters. They had long legs, short arms, and long heavy tails. But the most extraordinary thing about them was their big bizarre-looking skulls.

**STYGIMOLOCH**
(stih-jee-MOH-lock)
**When:** Late Cretaceous, 70-65 million years ago
**Where:** Montana
- Rounded dome with bumps, horns, and spikes
- Weighed 120 pounds— about the same as a large wolf

*Stygimoloch's amazing horns and spikes were just for show. This bone-head probably used its fancy headdress to attract mates and scare off rivals.*

# The Age of Dinosaurs

*Dinosaurs walked the earth during the Mesozoic era, also known as the Age of Dinosaurs. The Mesozoic era lasted from about 250 million to 65 million years ago. It is divided into three periods: the Triassic, Jurassic, and Cretaceous.*

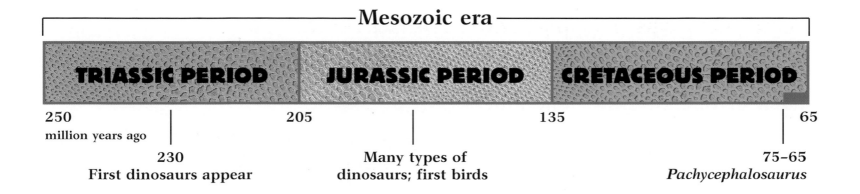

The bone-heads had an unusually thick layer of bone on top of their skulls. On some of the dinosaurs, the thickened skull was flat. On others it was rounded like a crash helmet. Some types of bone-heads also had bony knobs, horns, or spikes on their heads and snouts.

One of the most unusual skullcaps belonged to *Stygimoloch*. Long horns and spikes made this bone-headed dinosaur look like a movie monster. But like the rest of its cousins, *Stygimoloch* was basically a peaceful plant-eater.

# DOME-HEADED GIANT

*Pachycephalosaurus* was the largest bone-headed dinosaur. It measured about fifteen feet long—about the length of a large car. This giant's skull had a bony dome more than ten inches thick. That is twenty times thicker than a human skull! Bony knobs and spikes decorated the back of its skull and its snout.

A big head does not necessarily mean a big brain. In fact, *Pachycephalosaurus*'s brain was no bigger than a doughnut hole. But this bone-head had sharp senses to help it survive in the dinosaur world.

## EARLY-WARNING SYSTEM

*Pachycephalosaurus* had a tiny brain but plenty of good sense—or senses. Its fossils show that the part of its brain used for smelling was large. It also had big eyes that faced partly forward instead of sideways. Forward-facing eyes let an animal judge distances accurately.

*Pachycephalosaurus* lived in a dangerous world, with many fierce meat-eating neighbors. Its sharp eyes and good sense of smell helped it detect danger early. That way it could get a head start on its enemies and make a safe getaway.

**PACHYCEPHALOSAURUS**
(pak-ee-sef-ah-loh-SORE-us)
**When:** Late Cretaceous,
75-65 million years ago
**Where:** Alberta, Canada
◆ About 4 feet high at the hips;
weighed about 2 tons
◆ Name means "thick-headed lizard"

*The bone-headed dinosaurs were named for* Pachycephalosaurus, *the biggest of the group and one of the last to walk the earth.*

# A GOLDEN AGE

The Cretaceous period is sometimes called the "golden age of dinosaurs." That is because more kinds of dinosaurs lived in that time than ever before. One reason was the world's changing face. At the beginning of the Age of Dinosaurs, all the lands on earth were joined together in one huge supercontinent. Over many centuries, that landmass broke up and the pieces drifted apart. Many new kinds of dinosaurs developed on these big isolated "islands."

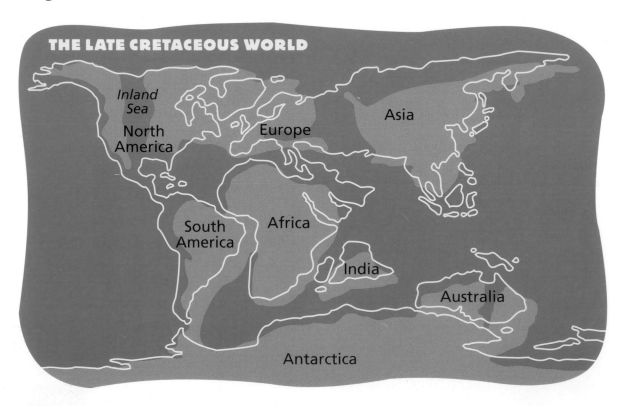

*By the Late Cretaceous period, the shifting continents were beginning to take their modern shape. The yellow outlines on this map show the shape of the modern continents; the green shading shows their position around 65 million years ago.*

*Many different kinds of plants flourished in the warm temperatures and abundant rainfall of the Late Cretaceous period.*

# CRETACEOUS NEIGHBORS

Let's take a trip back in time to the Late Cretaceous period. We land in the part of North America that one day will be Alberta, Canada. The ground is covered with green ferns, small shrubs, tall evergreens, and brightly colored flowering plants.

Many plant-eaters enjoy this endless salad bar. *Pachycephalosaurus* shares the feast with its bone-headed cousin *Stegoceras*. We might also

> **STEGOCERAS**
> (steg-uh-SEE-rus)
> **When:** Late Cretaceous, 75-70 million years ago
> **Where:** Alberta, Canada; and Montana
> ◆ Rounded dome with bony knobs around back of skull
> ◆ About the size of a goat

Stegoceras *uses its crash-helmet head to scare an intruder away from its nest.*

Albertosaurus, *the "Alberta lizard," was one of the most fearsome predators of Late Cretaceous North America.*

see herds of duck-billed dinosaurs with colorful head crests. There are horned dinosaurs like *Triceratops* and armored giants like *Ankylosaurus*. These plant-eaters sometimes become meals themselves. The king of the meat-eating dinosaurs is *Tyrannosaurus*, but sharp-fanged *Albertosaurus* can be just as fierce and dangerous.

# THE BONE-HEAD HERD

**HOMALOCEPHALE**
(ho-mah-loh-SEF-uh-lee)
**When:** Late Cretaceous,
  80-70 million years ago
**Where:** Mongolia
- Flat dome with rows of
  bony knobs
- About the size of a large lion

*Bone-heads may have lived in herds for protection from predators. One member of this* Homalocephale
*herd is taking a nap, while another keeps an eye out for danger.*

**M**any paleontologists (scientists who study prehistoric life) think that *Pachycephalosaurus* may have lived in small groups or herds. The herds spent most of their time eating. Roaming across the flat valleys and rocky hills of Alberta, they looked for tasty plants. The dinosaurs' small sharp teeth were not much good for chewing tough food. Instead, the bone-heads may have looked for soft leaves, seeds, and fruit.

While they ate, herd members kept watch for predators. They sniffed the air. They looked and listened. At the first sign of danger, they ran as fast as they could, with their heads down and their tails held out stiffly behind.

**GOYOCEPHALE**
(goy-uh-SEF-uh-lee)
**When:** Late Cretaceous,
85-80 million years ago
**Where:** Mongolia
♦ Flat dome with bony knobs
♦ Long pointed teeth in front of jaws, possibly for self-defense

Goyocephale *searched for low-growing plants in the dry upland plains of Mongolia. Like all bone-heads, it walked on two legs, with its back nearly level to the ground.*

## A QUESTION ON COMBAT

What if a meat-eater got so close that the pachycephalosaurs could not run to safety? Would they fight back with their thick skulls, like the bone-headed dinosaur at the beginning of this book? Some paleontologists say yes. They think a desperate bone-head might ram an attacker to injure it or scare it away.

Some scientists also believe the bone-heads used their crash-helmet heads against each other. The males sparred to decide who would lead the herd and mate with the females. In these contests two males faced off. Each lowered its head, stretched out its neck, and charged. The two skulls crashed together again and again. Finally, one dinosaur gave up and staggered away. The one with the thicker, stronger skull was the winner.

**PRENOCEPHALE**
(preh-no-SEF-uh-lee)
**When:** Late Cretaceous,
75-70 million years ago
**Where:** Mongolia
◆ Smooth rounded dome with
wreath of bony bumps
◆ Large forward-facing eyes

*Some paleontologists believe bone-heads like* Prenocephale *used their thick rounded skulls in head-butting contests. Flexible neck muscles and an extra-strong backbone might have worked like a car's shock absorbers to prevent serious injuries.*

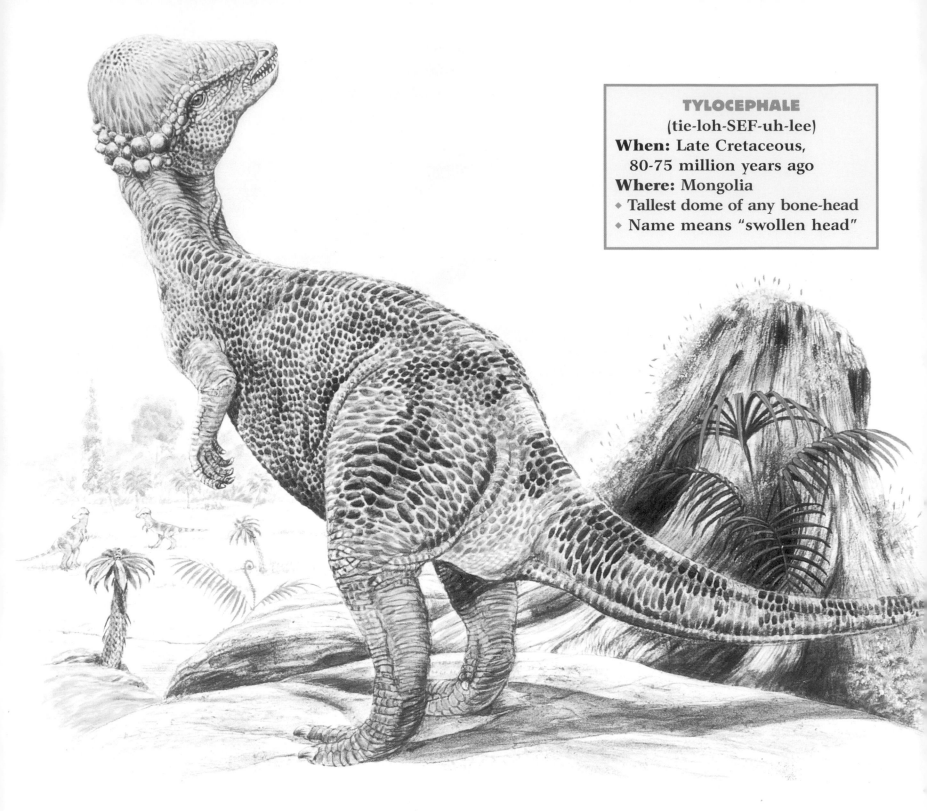

*A crownlike circle of bony knobs decorated* Tylocephale's *tall dome.*

Other paleontologists believe the bone-heads' skulls were too fragile for head-to-head combat. They point out that modern head-butting animals such as bighorn sheep have air spaces in their skulls to absorb knockout blows. The bone-heads did not. If they smashed their heavy heads together, they could be seriously injured, maybe even killed.

Instead, these scientists say, the bone-heads may have fought standing still. Joining heads, they pushed and shoved to see which was stronger. Or they might butt each other in the ribs, not head-on. In these less violent matches, there was still a winner and a loser, but both dinosaurs got a chance to live on and fight some other day.

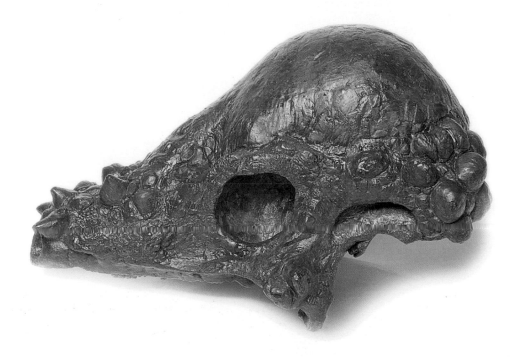

*A huge dome made of bone protected* Pachycephalosaurus's *tiny brain.*

The bizarre-looking bone-heads were one of the last groups of dinosaurs on earth. They lived in North America, Asia, Europe, and Africa from 110 to 65 million years ago.

# BONE-HEAD MYSTERIES

*Pachycephalosaurus* survived right up to the end of the Cretaceous period, about 65 million years ago. Then all the dinosaurs became extinct, or died out. No one knows what killed them. One idea is that a huge asteroid hit the earth, raising a cloud of dust that blocked the sun. The plants died, then the plant-eaters, and finally the meat-eating dinosaurs.

Very few bone-head fossils have ever been found. There is still much that paleontologists do not know about these unusual dinosaurs. What was life like in a *Pachycephalosaurus* herd? How did the dinosaurs take care of their babies? Did they really use their bizarre-looking skulls in head-to-head combat? Scientists are still searching for answers to all these puzzling questions about the incredible bone-headed dinosaurs.

# Dinosaur Family Tree

**ORDER**
All dinosaurs are divided into two large groups, based on the shape and position of their hipbones. Ornithischians had backward-pointing hipbones.

**SUBORDER**
Marginocephalians were plant-eating dinosaurs with a narrow shelf or deep bony frill at the back of the skull.

**INFRAORDER**
Pachycephalosaurs were two-legged plant-eaters with large, thickened skull bones.

**FAMILY**
A family includes one or more types of closely related dinosaurs.

**GENUS**
Every dinosaur has a two-word name. The first word tells us what genus, or type, of dinosaur it is. The genus plus the second word are its species—the group of very similar animals it belongs to. (For example, *Pachycephalosaurus wyomingensis* is one species of *Pachycephalosaurus*.)

Scientists organize all living things into groups, according to features shared.
This chart shows the groupings of the bone-headed plant-eaters in this book.

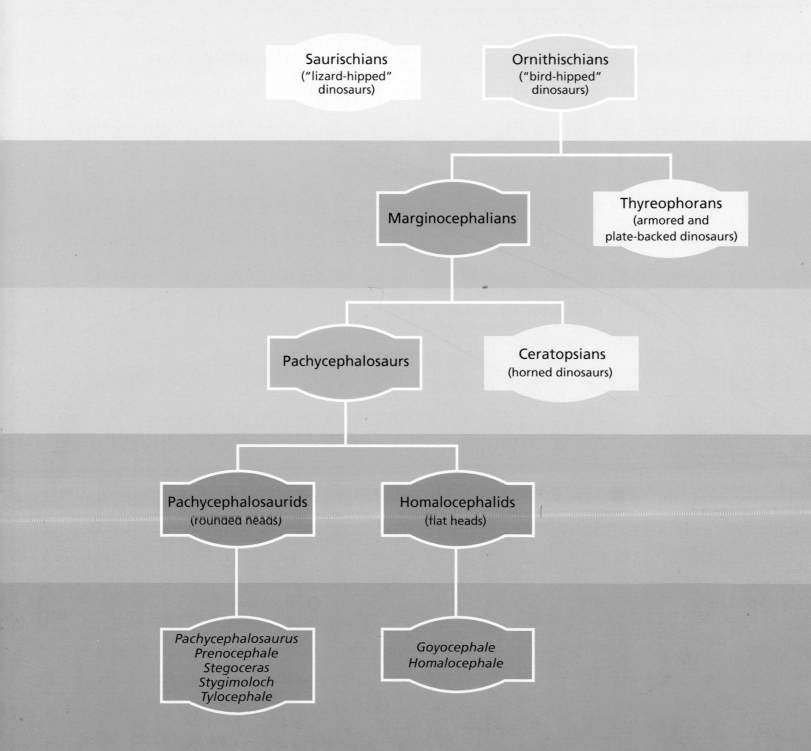

Saurischians
("lizard-hipped"
dinosaurs)

Ornithischians
("bird-hipped"
dinosaurs)

Marginocephalians

Thyreophorans
(armored and
plate-backed dinosaurs)

Pachycephalosaurs

Ceratopsians
(horned dinosaurs)

Pachycephalosaurids
(rounded heads)

Homalocephalids
(flat heads)

*Pachycephalosaurus*
*Prenocephale*
*Stegoceras*
*Stygimoloch*
*Tylocephale*

*Goyocephale*
*Homalocephale*

# Glossary

*Albertosaurus:* one of North America's most common tyrannosaurs, which lived from about 80 million to 65 million years ago

**asteroid:** a very small planet or fragment of a planet orbiting the sun

**Cretaceous** (krih-TAY-shus) **period:** the time period from about 135 million to 65 million years ago, when *Pachycephalosaurus* and most of the other bone-headed dinosaurs lived

**duck-billed dinosaurs:** a group of plant-eating dinosaurs with bulky bodies, long flat beaks, and sometimes distinctive head crests; also called hadrosaurs

**extinct:** no longer existing; an animal is extinct when every one of its kind has died

**fossils:** the hardened remains or traces of animals or plants that lived many thousands or millions of years ago

**pachycephalosaurs** (pak-ee-SEF-ah-loh-sores): a group of two-legged plant-eating dinosaurs with large thickened skull bones, which lived mainly in the Late Cretaceous period

**predator:** an animal that hunts and kills other animals for food

*Triceratops:* a large three-horned plant-eating dinosaur that lived in North America 70 to 65 million years ago

**tyrannosaurs:** two-fingered meat-eating dinosaurs that included some of the largest predators that ever lived

# Find Out More

## BOOKS

Freedman, Frances. *Looking at Pachycephalosaurus.* Milwaukee: Gareth Stevens, 1995.

Holmes, Thom, and Laurie Holmes. *Armored, Plated, and Bone-Headed Dinosaurs.* Berkeley Heights, NJ: Enslow, 2002.

*The Humongous Book of Dinosaurs.* New York: Stewart, Tabori, and Chang, 1997.

Marshall, Chris, ed. *Dinosaurs of the World*. 11 vols. New York: Marshall Cavendish, 1999.

Parker, Steve. *The Age of the Dinosaurs.* Vol. 12, *The Last of the Dinosaurs.* Danbury, CT: Grolier Educational, 2000.

# On-Line Sources *

*Illinois State Geological Survey, GeoScience Education and Outreach Unit* at
**http://www.isgs.uiuc.edu/dinos/pachygifs.html**
See photos of bone-head fossils found at the Hell Creek Formation in South Dakota.
A link takes you to *Dino Russ's Lair*, an excellent site created by geologist Russ
Jacobson, which includes other links to organizations offering on-line dinosaur
information and art.

*Journey Through Time* at
**http://www.nhm.org/journey/prehist/ornitho/home.html**
This Web site of the Natural History Museum of Los Angeles County offers
photos and facts for *Pachycephalosaurus* and other dinosaurs.

*Zoom Dinosaurs* at **http://www.zoomdinosaurs.com**
This colorful site from Enchanted Learning Software includes a world of information on dinosaur-related topics: dinosaur myths, records, behavior, and fossils; dinosaur fact sheets; quizzes, puzzles, printouts, and crafts; tips on writing a
school report; and more.

*Web site addresses sometimes change. For more on-line sources, check with the media specialist at your local library.*

# Index

**Virginia Schomp** grew up in a quiet suburban town in northeastern New Jersey, where eight-ton duck-billed dinosaurs once roamed. In first grade she discovered that she loved books and writing, and in sixth grade she was named "class bookworm," because she always had her nose in a book. Today she is a freelance author who has written more than thirty books for young readers on topics including careers, animals, ancient cultures, and modern history. Ms. Schomp lives in the Catskill Mountain region of New York with her husband, Richard, and their son, Chip.